THE LORD'S PRAYER TURNED INSIDE OUT

Gospel Syllabus

by

William A. Cummins

THE LORD'S PRAYER TURNED INSIDE OUT
Gospel Syllabus

ISBN 978-0-9971381-1-5
Library of Congress Control Number 2016902163

Copyright © 2016 by William A. Cummins

CAI Publishing
807 Black Duck Drive
Port Orange, Florida 32127

Printed in the United States of America

Published by CAI Publishing
807 Black Duck Drive
Port Orange, Florida 32127-4726

Telephone orders: 1.386.383.5198
Website: http://www.caipublishing.net
Email: wacumminspub@gmail.com

Dear William Cummins,

Ms. Cindy Hurtado and I have read, reviewed, and discussed your in-depth study of the Lord's Prayer. We realized this subject is very close to your heart and found your convictions very interesting.

Conclusion: We believe that your text would be an excellent syllabus for a lay person or a man of the cloth to use as teaching and sermon material in the world today.

Conclusion: As we continued to have an in-depth discussion about the text, we asked ourselves what would Jesus say if he were standing in the room with us?

Dr. William J. Lockhart,
Adjunct Professor

DISCLAIMER

The purpose of this book is to make the Lord's Prayer your daily word; one that leads you into the sonship of God every soul seeks.

The sonship of God is not to be taken lightly. Anyone desiring to follow this path should call upon the Holy Spirit for understanding and prayerfully follow the guidance received.

The comments in this book are not attempts to redefine Scripture, but to fulfill it. Should legal or other expert assistance be desired please pursue such interests in other venues. The resources of competent scholars should be sought by anyone interested in more information.

Every effort has been made to make this book as accurate as possible. However, there may be typographical or content mistakes. Therefore, the text should be used only as a general guide and not as the ultimate source of information.

The author and publisher shall have no responsibility or liability to any person, directly or indirectly, for any problems or troubles alleged to have been caused by the information in this book.

If you do not wish to be bound by the above, you may return this book to the publisher for a full refund.

CONTENTS

INTRODUCTION

Most people mindlessly recite the Lord's Prayer like parrots without regard for Jesus' warning about vain repetitions, not realizing the prayer contains the whole Christ Message.

Our goal is revealed in Romans 8:14: "For as many as are led by the Spirit of God, they are the sons (and daughters) of God." The sons and daughters of God walk daily upon His Word in faith.

The Lord's Prayer should convince everyone that the heart of the Creator which is the heart of God the Father is emotionally involved in His Kingdom.

I began to walk faithfully upon God's spoken word every day after attending John Shephard's classes and receiving a set of his *MANNA NOTES* in April of 1959. (See review.)

This syllabus is my personal journey into the Lord's Prayer and into the mind of God.

One morning, after reciting the Lord's Prayer, God asked, "My son, do you understood the prayer you just recited?" I responded, "I think so." Then He asked, "Can you explain it to me using different words?" I quickly admitted I could not.

During the last two years, while praying before rising each morning, I have discussed with God the seven petitions hidden within the Lord's Prayer. The on-going revelations of these discussions are always churning in my thoughts.

Turning the Lord's Prayer inside out is much like turning your pocket inside out. You first remove the contents and then reach in and pull the bottom of the pocket up through the top. Everything hidden inside now becomes visible for all to see. So, let's get started.

The Lord's Prayer turned inside out is a cosmic bomb. When cracked open the secrets of the world explode and change us forever. With this prayer, Jesus showed us how to pray as faithful sons and daughters of God in order to fully equip us for our earthly tasks of leading and healing.

Within the vast library of Christian documents the Lord's Prayer is by far the most important. It was designed by Jesus to keep the teaching of Christ's message simple and pure.

This Prayer is the greatest common denominator in all of the Christian Churches. Jesus constructed it very carefully with very clear goals in mind. Without exception, everyone who seeks to follow God's Way should pray it daily.

The Lord's Prayer is the spiritual anchor holding mankind in place as it learns to trust, verify, and follow the words of the living God. Jesus the Christ smiles when we look beyond Him and see God the Father in all His glory.

TWO LORD'S PRAYERS

Jesus gave his followers this fundamental Christian prayer in response to his disciples' request, "Lord, teach us to pray."

God's desires and the power of His word are revealed in the Lord's Prayer. The insights enable his followers to faithfully offer God's love to all of His people.

The Holy Bible contains two versions of the Lord's Prayer produced by different writers. They are found in the book of Matthew and the book of Luke.

Printed below are both versions as written in the King James Version of the Holy Bible:

Matthew 6:9-13 (66 words)

Our Father which art in heaven, Hallowed be thy name. Thy kingdom come. Thy will be done in earth, as it is in heaven. Give us this day our daily bread. And forgive us our debts, as we forgive our debtors. And lead us not into temptation, but deliver us from evil: For thine is the kingdom, and the power, and the glory, for ever. Amen.

Luke 11:2-4 (58 words)

Our Father which art in heaven, Hallowed be thy name. Thy kingdom come. Thy will be done, as in heaven, so in earth. Give us day by day our daily bread. And forgive us our sins; for we also forgive every one that is indebted to us. And lead us not into temptation; but deliver us from evil.

Albert Einstein said, "Everything should be made as simple as possible and not one bit simpler." The Lord's Prayer is truly the summary of the Gospel.

In teaching us to pray, Jesus presents himself as our model. He invites us to become his disciples and to follow him. In humbling himself he has given us an example to imitate when we address our Father in heaven.

The Lord's Prayer is said by billions of people every day in every language on the planet. The prayer was made powerful for a reason. Its words shape individual lives and families and communities and whole societies. .

The first words we learn as children and the last words we say at the moment of death are in the Lord's Prayer. All scripture from creation to the covenants, law, grace, faith, hope, love, sonship, and death itself, has been fulfilled in Christ.

The single most important message gleaned from the Lord's Prayer is this. Jesus wanted to lead us to His loving Father and died to accomplish that task!

PRAYER MAKES US HUMAN

We become human when we invite God to come into our problems and situations and to work on them with us.

In Genesis we glimpse man as God pictured him from the beginning. He is a son of God partaking of divine nature and ministering the love and justice of God to all creatures.

"So God created man in His image.... and God blessed them, and said unto them, 'Be fruitful and multiply, and replenish the earth and subdue it: and have dominion... over every living thing that moveth upon the earth'." Genesis 1:27-28.

When Jesus called the disciples to follow him, each one had to **stop** what he was doing, **look** at Jesus, and **listen** to him. By giving us the Lord's Prayer Jesus reveals the same three steps are required by us as we fulfill our destiny.

Every human is unique, having different physical, mental, and spiritual skills and needs. We were created male and female to become sons and daughters of God with the power to determine our destiny with our thoughts. We will produce in our experience what we think about and dwell upon.

While analyzing the Lord's Prayer it became evident that Jesus spoke in modern day sound-bites. And these sound-bites can easily be understood by using bullet points.

We will utilize these streams of thought as we look at Matthew's version of the Lord's Prayer. The sound-bites of Jesus are listed first, bolded, and italicized, followed by bullet points.

The words underlined and bolded in the bullet points represent the seven petitions we request God do for us during the prayer:

1. Our Father which art in heaven, Hallowed be thy name.

- We ask God to **<u>remind</u>** us of who He is, where He is, and what He is.
- Our Father reminds us we were created in God's image and likeness.
- God dwells in heaven while we live on earth as His sons and daughters.
- Hallowed reminds us God's name means total and complete.

2. Thy kingdom come.

- God's kingdom comes when the Holy Spirit **<u>enables</u>** us with power from on high.
- Jesus displayed this mighty power from on high as he healed, performed miracles, commanded the elements, and fulfilled his destiny as the first born Son of the Father.

- Enabled with nine supernatural abilities at Pentecost, mankind's task is to accomplish God's work in our earthly vessels as sons and daughters of God.

3. Thy will be done in earth, as it is in heaven.

- We ask God to **inspire** to do what is good, and right, and true, as in heaven.
- Discernment of God's will is from the Holy Spirit— Not my will, but thy will be done.
- Doing God's will means to wholeheartedly love him and to act accordingly.

4. Give us this day our daily bread.

- We ask God to **feed** us daily with so many blessings from the storehouse in heaven we cannot contain them all.
- These blessings cover all aspect of our lives including our spiritual, mental, physical, financial, social, and emotional needs.

5. And forgive us our debts, as we forgive our debtors.

- We ask God to **forgive** our human debts and transgressions as we forgive others.
- To achieve this we need the same forgiving spirit within us that was displayed by Jesus on the cross when he said, "Father, forgive them for they know not what they do."

- God places the judgment of our actions back upon us by giving us the power to forgive others which fulfills our destiny as sons and daughters of God.

6. And lead us not into temptation,

- We ask God to **lead** us away from our own carnal desires of lust, greed, and pride.
- Jesus had to overcome these three basic human desires during his 40 days in the wilderness before he began His ministry.

7. But deliver us from evil,

- We ask God to **deliver** us from evil, which reveals our helplessness against evil.
- As humans we wrestle not against flesh and blood, but against principalities, against powers, against the rulers of the darkness of this world, against spiritual wickedness in high places.
- Any attempt to challenge and overcome the power of evil by ourselves is doomed.
- This is the domain of God who has given us the power to identify evil, bind it, and cast it into outer darkness for all eternity, in the name of Jesus the Christ.

8. For thine is the kingdom, and the power, and the glory, forever. Amen.

- The last prayer verse is not a petition.

• This verse is an acknowledgment of God's dominion over the entire universe. So be it.

God is the Father who wants His children to talk with Him honestly and sincerely and to cast all our cares and dreams upon Him.

Prayer is simply a conversation with God. It is seeking His word to meet our needs followed by praise and thanksgiving.

SEVEN PRAYER PETITIONS

Upon receiving God's guidance with the Lord's Prayer, I realized Jesus had organized the heart of his prayer with seven key words.

I found myself returning to these words each time I recited the prayer. These words, bolded and underlined in the previous bullet points, are expanded here:

Remind us loving creator of mankind as you dwell in the holy realm, that your name means total and complete.

Enable us with power from on high through your Holy Spirit to heal, perform miracles, and command the elements as your faithful sons and daughters.

Inspire us with your desires to do what is good, and right, and true, in our earthly realm as it is in your holy realm.

Feed us spiritually, mentally, physically, financially, socially, and emotionally each day with so many blessing from the storehouse of heaven we cannot contain them all. And

Forgive us our debts and transgressions against you by giving us the forgiving spirit of Jesus so we may forgive those with debts and transgressions against us. And

Lead us away from our carnal desires of lust, greed, and pride by giving us words of power to defend us when tempted, just as Jesus defeated the persuasions of the devil in the wilderness, but

Deliver us from evil on our journey through life because we wrestle not against flesh and blood, but against principalities, against powers, against the rulers of the darkness of this world, against spiritual wickedness in high places.

The **Kingdom** is an essential truth that God is a manifestation or expression. We know God is the **Power** and mankind is his fingers. Gradually we realize the **Glory** and the majesty of God in our lives and the bliss we receive in that experience passes on to God himself.

The Lord's Prayer can be turned inside out by adding understanding and expression to these seven key words.

When we pray to the living Father, his divine intelligence works through us to accomplish his purposes.

My journey into the Lord's Prayer has not been influenced by anyone but God himself through His Holy Spirit. Let your mind flow freely as you attach your own thoughts to each key word.

NINE SUPERNATURAL GIFTS

Jesus said to the disciple at the last supper, "Nevertheless I tell you the truth; It is expedient for you that I go away: for if I go not away, the Comforter will not come unto you; but if I depart, I will send him unto you." (John 16:7).

The good news is the Comforter, which is the Holy Ghost/Spirit, will come to take the place of Jesus in order to teach us more about Jesus.

In John 14:26 we see the commission of the Holy Spirit which was poured out at Pentecost:

"But the Comforter, which is the Holy Ghost, whom the Father will send in my name, he shall teach you all things, and bring all things to your remembrance, whatsoever I have said unto you."

The Holy Spirit is described as power from on high. In Luke 24:49 we see "And, behold, I send the promise of my Father upon you: but tarry ye in the city of Jerusalem, until ye be endued with power from on high."

God releases His power into every Spirit-filled Christian through nine supernatural abilities which are more popularly called gifts of the Spirit. For study purposes these gifts can be functionally separated into three categories:

Utterance or Worship Gifts

1. **Tongues** is speaking is a spiritual language which unlocks all the supernatural abilities in your life.
2. **Interpretation** lets the mind express in a known language what is spoken in tongues.
3. **Prophecy** is utterance in a known language under the inspiration of the Holy Spirit.

Revelation Gifts

4. **Discerning of spirits** is the ability to distinguish between good spirits and evil spirits.
5. **Word of knowledge** is information given to us by God for enlightenment.
6. **Word of wisdom** is guidance or direction as to how to act in light of spiritual information.

Power Gifts

7. **Faith** is taking appropriate action based upon God's Living Word in manifestation.
8. **Miracles** are manifestations that contradict our understanding of natural physical order.
9. **Healing** depends upon the hearer's ability to believe God's Word into manifestation.

At least one of these nine abilities can be used for the benefit of all believers, but it is the same God who inspires them all in everyone.

These supernatural gifts are the spiritual power given to the saints of God to perform their mission.

POWER OF CLEAVING

This power first appeared in Genesis 2:24 when God united Adam and Eve in marriage saying, "Therefore shall a man leave his father and his mother, and shall cleave unto his wife: and they shall be one flesh."

My highly acclaimed book, *Life Is Sexually Transmitted Marriage—Why Marriage Is All About Cleaving,*" focuses on why the man must cleave unto his wife.

Although considered among the best marriage handbooks, it delved only briefly into the ending of the verse: "and they shall be one flesh."

So let's take a look at it. The word cleaving has two opposite meanings: 1) to separate, and 2) to go into and stay. For this journey it means, 'to go into and stay.'

Conception occurred when the living seed of Adam cleaved unto the ovum of Eve. This produced Abel, their first son. The amazing power of cleaving was demonstrated when Adam's seed penetrated the ovum, went into it, and stayed.

The questions now become, "Why must the man cleave unto his wife, and why did God use cleaving to reproduce life?" Let's look again at the beginning of mankind in Genesis.

In Genesis 1:26-27 God said, "Let us make man in <u>our</u> image, after our likeness:" In Genesis 2:7, it records, "And the Lord God fashioned man of the dust of the ground, and breathed into his nostrils the <u>breath of life</u>, and man became a living soul."

Within these verses we perceive a glimpse of God's absolute brilliance!

God's breath of life first cleaved unto Adam through his nostrils. God then enabled Adam to produce living seed that could physically leave his body. Adam's seed was given the honor of carrying within it God's breath of life.

When Adam's living seed cleaved unto the ovum of Eve, it released God's breath of life and ignited the living soul of a new generation.

How, you ask, does cleaving relate to the Lord's Prayer? The answer is simple.

Jesus constructed within the Lord's Prayer the essence of God's word. When God's word is heard by a willing soul, faith is imparted which enables the Holy Spirit to transform the person.

When God's word cleaves unto the soul of man by faith, it ignites the spirit within and a new man is conceived. The old man passes away and a new man is born not of flesh and blood, but of the Spirit.

As you can now see, cleaving is essential for the bonding of man to God, a man to his wife, the birth of a baby, and the rebirth of a man through faith.

It is time to reclaim the power of cleaving in our Christian experience, teaching, and preaching.

WHAT DOES IT MEAN?

Jesus taught the Lord's Prayer to his disciples and to future generations in order to build a solid foundation for our new lives as sons and daughters.

Becoming human begins when the ear has heard the Word of God proclaimed. This is followed by illumination from the Holy Spirit when the eye actually perceives God's grace.

The believing heart understands only as the full implication of God's Word is grasped. It is through the lips that we express what is in the heart. The challenge of the Lord's Prayer is for us to become DOERS of God's Word and not hearers only.

Being a DOER means when the new man with Christ within hears the Word, "The Lord is my shepherd, I shall not want," he lays hold of the Word in the face of lack and insecurity. This new man is now a follower who UNDERSTANDS.

God's Spirit came to me after reading only two verses alone from a small Gideon Bible when I was 20 years old. When I said a short prayer it cracked open the window of my soul and God rushed in. It's true, "Prayer changes everything."

During prayer we learn how to walk and talk with God. Our thoughts become a conversation much like the lyrics in the great old hymn entitled, "In The Garden":

"I come to the garden alone while the dew is still on the roses, and the voice I hear falling on my ear, the Son of God discloses. And he walks with me, and he talks with me, and he tells me I am his own; and the joy we share as we tarry there, none other has ever known."

The seventh and last petition in the Lord's Prayer is for God to "Deliver us from evil." After repeating the Lord's Prayer each morning I often put on the armor of God for protection from evil by paraphrasing Ephesians 6:13-17:

"Father God; Gird me with truth through the Christ within; Cover me with the breastplate of righteousness through the Christ within; Shoe my feet with the preparation of the gospel of peace through the Christ within; Give me the shield of faith to quench all the fiery darts of the wicked through the Christ within; Cover my head with the helmet of salvation through the Christ within; And finally give me the sword of the Spirit, which is the word of the living God, through the Christ within. Having done all, teach me to stand upon all the work that Jesus has done; All the victories He has won; And all the love, hope, and faith He has begun. Thank you, Father. Amen."

Please consult God about the meaning of the Lord's Prayer for your own daily walk. Ask the Holy Spirit of God to lead you into sonship.

REVIEW OF *MANNA NOTES*

MANNA NOTES—Foundations for the New Life is a Christian Treasure Trove written by John Shephard in 1959 for students of his classes.

It is a timeless book of infinite value! It will inspire and change your life by empowering you with the sonship of God every soul seeks.

Compiled into *MANNA NOTES* are the twelve original studies written by John Shephard. His notes are preserved in this book which is unlike any work you have ever seen.

This syllabus goes hand in hand with John's writings. Since attending John's classes in April, 1959, I have lived my life as a son of God and was led to release the book, MANNA NOTES, in 2016.

In 1962 the Bethel Methodist Church members in Columbus, Ohio, began to live, teach, and preach John's foundations for the new life.

As the Spirit of God spread outward attendance grew and a Columbus police officer was assigned to direct traffic during the Sunday Church service.

The young adult Pillars Sunday School Class at Bethel Methodist Church in 1962 was a diverse group of farmers, builders, teachers, professors, engineers, and others who studied the Bible.

The power of the Holy Spirit bonded the class together so strongly it still holds annual reunions decades later.

Ann's Testimony

I read '*MANNA NOTES*' while alone in a quiet room in our home. After finishing I began to cry. I looked up to Heaven and said, "I don't understand the tears, Lord," but the tears still flowed.

I thought to myself, "Bill will know why I'm crying." So I went into his office with tissue in hand. My husband was seated at the computer and looked up to see me in tears. I cried even harder when he stood up and took me in his comforting arms.

He wanted to know what was wrong... but of course there was nothing wrong. When I told him what had happened he was thrilled and said, "I'm so happy I don't know what to do. God gently touched your heart when the book revealed how much He loves you."

I understand now that the notes had touched me deeply, and joy had poured forth as tears. I highly recommend '*MANNA NOTES*' to everyone... because if this can happen to me, it can also happen to you.

Ann L. Cummins, Port Orange, Florida

The purpose of *MANNA NOTES* is to teach everyone how to walk and talk with God as sons and daughters led by His Spirit.

OTHER BOOKS BY AUTHOR WILLIAM A. CUMMINS

LIFE IS SEXUALLY TRANSMITTED—Why Marriage Is All About Cleaving.
A marriage handbook about love and advice for matrimony.

THE FORGOTTEN—Volume One—The Forgotten Flag; The Forgotten War; The Forgotten Victory.
Award-winning book of foxhole stories told in the Veterans' own words.

KING and the COWBOY—The Saga of Smilin' Bill and His Wonder Horse King.
True story of Bill Cummins who lived every little boy's dream.

MANNA NOTES—Foundations for the New Life
This inspirational book empowers you with the sonship of God every soul seeks.

These books are 'timeless and priceless' and come with a 100% satisfaction guarantee.

Signed books are precious treasures which can be ordered from the publisher at: *http://www. caipublishing.net.*

Please tell your friends. By prayer and word of mouth, these books will circle the globe.

CAI Publishing
807 Black Duck Drive, Suite A
Port Orange, FL 32127
Call: 386-383-5198